SCHOLASTIC

50 Fill-in Math Word Problems

GRADES 2–3

BY BOB KRECH

NEW YORK • TORONTO • LONDON • AUCKLAND • SYDNEY
MEXICO CITY • NEW DELHI • HONG KONG • BUENOS AIRES

Teaching *Resources*

Dedication

Thanks to Andrew and Faith for laughing.

Thanks to Jean Davis's fourth graders at Millstone River School, Plainsboro, New Jersey, for their helpful feedback.

Edited by Joan Novelli
Cover and interior design by Holly Grundon
Interior illustrations by Mike Gordon and Mike Moran

ISBN-13: 978-0-439-51188-9 / ISBN-10: 0-439-51188-7

Contents

About This Book 4

What Are Fill-in Math Word Problems? 4

Why Use Fill-in Math Word Problems? 4

Meeting the Math Standards 4

Choosing Numbers and Checking Answers 5

How to Use Fill-in Math Word Problems 6

Teaching Problem-Solving Skills:
The Fantastic Five-Step Process 6

Fill-in Math Word Problems

Number and Operations . . . 10

Old Folktale 11

Sports Update. 12

Alien Love 13

The Author. 14

The Three Brothers. 15

Garden News. 16

Taking Care of Your Teeth . . . 17

Directions to My House. 18

My Collection 19

Pet Care. 20

Crime Report. 21

Historical Site. 22

My Allowance 23

Holiday!. 24

Birthday Money. 25

Garage Sale 26

My Favorite Restaurant. 27

History Report 28

Going Shopping. 29

Secret Agent X 30

Arms of Steel 31

The Cousins' Visit 32

Organizing My Room 33

Candy 34

Pizza Dinner 35

Measurement. 36

Guide to the Famous Tower . . 37

An Incredible Find! 38

The TV Guide 39

Doing Homework 40

What a Chore!. 41

How to Build a
_____ball Court 42

Arts and Crafts 43

A Cool Drink. 44

Bake a Cake 45

Pirate Gold. 46

Geometry 47

The Garden. 48

Hat Shopping 49

The Sculpture 50

Chef Bob's Creation 51

The New Playground. 52

Patterns and Algebra 53

Message From the Cave 54

Aliens Speak! 55

Big Winner 56

The Big Sale 57

The Scientific Lecture. 58

**Data Analysis
and Probability** 59

Soccer Stars 60

The Contest 61

Baseball Hero 62

The Probability _____ 63

County Fair. 64

About This Book

When we learn to read, we learn to recognize the letters of the alphabet, we practice letter-sound relationships, and we learn punctuation, but what it's all about is eventually being able to read text. A similar situation exists in math. We learn how to recognize and write numerals, what the symbols mean, numerical order, and operations like addition and subtraction, but what it's all about is what you can do with these skills—applying what you know to solve problems. Fill-in math word problems provide some *very* interesting problems to solve.

What Are Fill-in Math Word Problems?

A fill-in math word problem is a funny math story waiting to happen. Most of the word problem is already supplied, except for a few key words and numbers that have been removed and replaced with blanks. It's up to students to fill in those blanks with missing nouns, verbs, and adjectives—just as they would in other word games. The difference is that this game is missing some numbers as well. When your students supply the missing numbers along with the words, you suddenly have a wacky math word problem that's fun to read and solve!

Why Use Fill-in Math Word Problems?

Math word problems can provide a meaningful context for students to apply their skills, but sometimes the problems can be a bit boring or dry. (Remember trying to figure out when the two trains would pass each other?) That won't happen with fill-in math word problems. Students help create these problems, and once they get the hang of the process, the resulting word problems become more and more wild, interesting, and fun—all while providing good problem-solving practice with grade-appropriate math skills and concepts. Have fun while doing math? Absolutely!

Meeting the Math Standards

To make it easy to select stories that correspond to the math skills you are teaching, this book is organized by content standards. The first 25 stories correspond to the Number and Operations standard, the next 10 to the Measurement standard, followed by 5 each for Geometry, Patterns and Algebra, and Data Analysis and Probability. The stories within each section are arranged by level of concept difficulty—for example, stories for Number and Operations begin with simple comparisons of numbers, followed by single-digit addition, addition with three addends, subtraction, work with double digits, money, multiplication, and division. You can follow the order in the book or select problems based on concepts you are teaching at a given time.

Choosing Numbers and Checking Answers

Some fill-in math word problems specify a range for numbers—for example, Arms of Steel (page 31) specifies a one-digit number, while Taking Care of Your Teeth (page 17) asks for two-digit numbers. Other stories, such as Old Folktale (page 11), invite children to fill in three-digit numbers. Some, such as Organizing My Room (page 33), simply ask for a number, any number. You may choose to let students fill in numbers according to the directions in the stories, or you can tighten the parameters to provide for differentiation of instruction, individualizing the problems for students by using the number ranges that make sense for them. (For example, instead of leaving the direction at "a three-digit number," you might substitute "a three-digit number between 100 and 200.") However, keep in mind that leaving the number size open-ended is an interesting option, and will provide information about students' ability to work with different-size numbers. There is no answer key for fill-in math word problems since answers will vary depending on the numbers students supply to fill in the blanks. You might set up a buddy system for checking answers, or have students turn in their stories for you to check.

Types of Words

Different kinds of words are required to fill in the blanks of the math problems. Following are the main types students will use. Review them and consider posting the descriptions and examples for easy reference.

Adjectives: Words that describe something, such as *smelly, happy, fierce, silly,* and *huge*

Adverbs: Words that tell how something is done, such as *quickly, sadly, sleepily,* and *carefully*

Exclamations: Words such as *ouch, yikes, wow,* and *oh*

Nouns: Words that name a person, place, or thing, such as *refrigerator, dog, book,* and *sandwich.* Sometimes plural nouns are asked for. This means more than one, such as *refrigerators, dogs, books,* and *sandwiches.*

Verbs: Action words like *run, catch, eat,* and *hop.* Sometimes past-tense verbs are asked for, such as *ran, caught, ate,* and *hopped.*

How to Use Fill-in Math Word Problems

There are many ways to use fill-in math word problems in your classroom. Here are a few suggestions for lesson formats:

Problem-Solving Partners: Have students pair up. Make copies of a fill-in math word problem and distribute to one student in each pair. These students are the Readers. Without revealing the title of the story (or the story), Readers ask their partners for the missing words in the order they appear in the story (for example, "a plural noun," "an adjective," "a two-digit number") and fill in the appropriate blanks with responses. When all the blanks are filled in, the Reader reads back the finished story. The resulting story now contains a math word problem. Partners work together to solve the problem and then share answers and strategies.

Class Problem Solvers: Choose a story and request the words or numbers in order from the class (students can also take over this role). Fill in the appropriate blanks with responses. When the story is complete, read it to the class. Have students take notes on the numbers used and the question being asked, or write this information on the chalkboard. Work together as a class to solve the problem.

Class Copies: After completing a story with class responses, make copies of the finished story for each student. Have students read the problem and solve it on their own. Write answers and solution strategies on the chalkboard and discuss.

Teaching Problem-Solving Skills: The Fantastic Five-Step Process

Problem solving is the first process standard listed in the NCTM *Principles and Standards for Mathematics Teaching 2000*. The accompanying statement reads "Problem solving should be the central focus of all mathematics instruction and an integral part of all mathematical activity." In other words, in mathematics, problem solving is what it's all about!

What do you do when you first encounter a math word problem? This is what we need to help students deal with. We need to help them develop a process that they can use effectively to solve any type of math word problem. Word problems often intimidate students because there may be a lot of information, what is there is embedded in text, and, unlike a regular equation, it is not always clear exactly what you are supposed to do. When using fill-in math word problems, you may want to take some time to teach students how to use the Fantastic Five-Step Process to problem solve.

The Fantastic Five-Step Process helps students approach problem solving in a logical, systematic way. No matter what type of problem students encounter, these five steps will help them through it. Learning and using the five steps will help students *organize* their interpretation and thinking about the problem. This is the key to good problem solving—organizing for action. The best way to help students understand the process is to demonstrate it as you work through a problem on the chalkboard or overhead. Make a copy of the graphic organizer on page 9. You can enlarge this to poster size, or provide each student with a copy to follow along as you take them through an introductory lesson.

Step 1: What Do I Know?

Begin by writing this problem on the board or overhead:

> Jock had 72 lima bean-flavored gumdrops in his candy jar.
> His brother, Jack, had 89. His sister, Jinx, had 98. Jinx said Jack
> had more than Jock. Is she right? If so, how many more?

Read the problem carefully. What are the facts? Have students volunteer these orally. Write them on the board.

> Jock had 72 gumdrops.
> Jack had 89 gumdrops.
> Jinx had 98 gumdrops.

Encourage students to write down the facts. This will help them focus on what is important while looking for ways to put it in a more accessible form. Can we arrange the facts in a way that will help us understand the problem situation? For instance, maybe it would be good to draw a picture of what we know, put it in a list, or make a table. Sometimes it's helpful to arrange numbers from lowest to highest or highest to lowest, especially if we are asked to compare. Are we being asked to compare? Yes!

> Jinx - 98
> Jack - 89
> Jock - 72

Step 2: What Do I Want to Know?

What is the question in the problem? What are we trying to find out? It is a good idea to have students state the question and also determine how the answer will be labeled. For example, if the answer is 72, then it's 72 what? 72 cats? 72 coins?

> We want to know two things:
> 1. Was Jinx right when she said Jack had more gumdrops than Jock?
>
> 2. How many more gumdrops does Jack have than Jock?

Step 3: What Can I Eliminate?

Once we know what we are trying to find out, we can decide what is unimportant. We may need all the information, but often there is extra information that can be put aside to help focus on the facts.

> We can eliminate the fact that Jinx had 98 gumdrops. It's not needed to answer the question. We're left with:

> Jack - 89
>
> Jock - 72

> By comparing the numbers, we can answer the first part of the question now. Jinx was right. Jack has more.

Step 4: Choose a Strategy or Action and Solve.

Is there an action in the story (for example, is something being "taken away" or is something being "shared") that will help us decide on an operation or a way to solve the problem?

> Since we have to compare something, we have to find the difference. Usually, the best way is to subtract or add. This is the action we need to do:

$$\begin{array}{r} 89 \\ -72 \\ \hline 17 \end{array}$$

> So Jack had 17 more gumdrops than Jock.

Step 5: Does My Answer Make Sense?

Reread the problem. Look at the answer. Is it reasonable? Is it a sensible answer given what we know?

> It makes sense. For one thing, 17 is a lower number than the higher number we started with. If it was higher, that would be a problem because the difference between two whole positive numbers cannot be higher than the highest number.

Try a number of different word problems using this "talk through" format with students. You can use sample problems from throughout the book. You might invite students to try the problem themselves first and then debrief step-by-step together, sharing solutions to see if all steps were considered and the solutions are, in fact, correct. Practicing the process in this way helps make it part of a student's way of thinking mathematically.

The Fantastic Five-Step Process

1. What do I KNOW?

2. What do I WANT TO KNOW?

3. What can I ELIMINATE?

4. Choose a STRATEGY or ACTION and SOLVE.

5. Does my answer MAKE SENSE?

Number and Operations

The fill-in math word problems in this section include math content that supports the math standards for number and operations across grades 2–3 (based on the *Principles and Standards for School Mathematics* from the National Council of Teachers of Mathematics) and are organized to accommodate the range of levels you would find in your class. As students complete the blanks in each story, they will build and solve word problems that provide practice in the following areas:

Understand numbers, ways of representing numbers, relationships among numbers, and number systems

★ count with understanding; recognize "how many"

★ place value and the base-ten number system

★ ordinal and cardinal numbers

★ relating, composing, and decomposing numbers

★ connect number words and numerals to the quantities they represent

★ understand and represent commonly used fractions

Understand meanings of operations and how they relate to one another

★ addition and subtraction of whole numbers

★ multiplication and division of whole numbers; equal groupings of objects and sharing equally

★ relationships between operations

★ properties of operations (such as the distributivity of multiplication over addition)

Compute fluently and make reasonable estimates

★ fluency in adding, subtracting, multiplying, and dividing whole numbers

★ use a variety of methods and tools to compute (such as objects, mental computation, estimation, paper and pencil, and calculators)

★ fluency with basic number combinations (with addition, subtraction, multiplication and division)

★ estimate the results of whole-number computations

Source: *Principles and Standards for School Mathematics* (National Council of Teachers of Mathematics, 2000); my.nctm.org

Tips for Teaching With This Section

$$\begin{array}{r} 3{,}180 \\ -\ 1{,}010 \\ \hline \end{array}$$

Share the following reminders with students to assist them in working with numbers:

★ Use commas in numbers with four or more digits to keep all those digits organized.

★ When comparing numbers—for example, to see which one is greater—write down the numbers one on top of the other, with the digits aligned, in order to make an accurate visual comparison.

★ When performing operations, align digits properly to avoid mistakes in computation.

★ When solving equations, check the final answer and ask yourself if it makes sense. (For more problem-solving strategies, see pages 7–8.) This "number sense" check helps. To do a good number-sense check, round the numbers in question, to get a good, reasonable estimate of what the answer should be. This provides a point of comparison to determine whether the actual answer does indeed make sense.

Name _____ Date _____

Old Folktale

This is an old _____ folktale from
(adjective)

_____. It seems there once was a queen named
(place)

_____. One day she declared, "Whoever can catch
(name of girl in the class)

the most _____ from the _____ forest
(plural noun)   (adjective)

will win my hand in marriage, as long as he catches more than

_____." Only two men accepted the challenge.
(three-digit number)

A woodcutter named _____ tried first. He caught
(name of boy in the class)

_____ by using a _____ with a long
(different three-digit number)   (noun)

handle. A _____ went next. Since he was
(occupation)

_____ and _____, he caught
(adjective)   (adjective)

_____ with a _____.
(different three-digit number)   (noun)

Question: Who got to marry the queen? _____

Name _____   Date _____

Sports Update

The National Target _____ Championships were held
(verb ending in -ing)

this past weekend. Competitors from all over _____ and
(place)

as far away as _____ attended. Defending champion
(place)

_____ went first. She was wearing her famous good luck
(name of girl)

_____ on her head. She scored _____. The
(noun)   (three-digit number)

lowest qualifying score of course is _____. Next came
(three-digit number)

that _____ challenger, _____. He shot
(adjective)   (name of boy)

a _____ using his trusty _____. Finally,
(three-digit number)   (noun)

newcomer _____ shot. The teacher's score was
(name of teacher)

_____.
(three-digit number)

Question: **Who won the competition?** _____

Name _____ Date _____

Alien Love

I love the girl from Planet

_____. She is so
(noun)

special! When I see her I say,

"_____," and I
(exclamation)

turn _____. I love her _____
(color)   (one-digit number)

_____ eyes. Her ears are so _____
(adjective)   (adjective)

and her hair is a stunning _____. She has
(color)

_____ fingers on her left hand and _____
(one-digit number)   (one-digit number)

on her right hand. She wears a ring made out of _____
(plural noun)

on each finger.

Question: How many rings does she wear? _____

Name _____   Date _____

The Author

I am writing a _____ new book about _____ .
             (adjective)   (plural noun)

My last book was about _____ in _____
                            (plural noun)   (place)

at the turn of the century. Everyone said it was _____ .
                                                     (adjective)

I am writing really _____ this time. I have been
                          (adverb)

writing for _____ days. On Saturday I started at
              (one-digit number)

_____ and wrote for two hours. I wrote _____
    (time)   (one-digit number)

pages. On Sunday I wrote _____ pages.
                          (one-digit number)

Question: How many pages did the author write this weekend? _____

Name _____   Date _____

The Three Brothers

There once were three brothers: _____,
                                      (first name of boy)

_____, and _____. They loved
   (name of male teacher)   (name of famous male athlete)

music, and each learned to play a unique instrument. The first

learned to play the _____. He would play
                             (noun)

_____ of them at the same time. The second
(one-digit number greater than 1)

learned to play the _____. He used
                             (noun)

_____ when he played. And the third learned the
   (one-digit number)

_____. He always used _____ when
        (noun)   (one-digit number)

performing. Together they formed a band. They called it the

_____ _____. The band was so famous
     (adjective)   (animal, plural)

they were even on _____.
                        (television show)

Question: How many instruments did they use in the band? _____

Name _____   Date _____

Garden News

_____ 's garden is doing very
(name of girl)

well this year. Unfortunately, last year the only

thing that grew were the _____,
(plural noun)

and they did not taste so good in the salad. But this year she

used plenty of _____ and _____ on
(liquid)   (plural noun)

the soil. She also _____ it every week. Of course,
(past-tense verb)

her favorite thing to grow is _____. They are just so
(plural noun)

_____. In June she picked _____ and
(adjective)   (one-digit number)

in July _____. In August she picked _____
(one-digit number)   (one-digit number)

more. They all tasted _____, especially with a little
(adjective)

_____ on top.
(noun)

Question: How many did she pick this summer? _____

Name _____ Date _____

Taking Care of Your Teeth

Taking good care of your teeth is

very important, so here are some

suggestions. Make sure you use a

good, _____
(adjective)

_____ to brush with.
(noun)

Also use a toothpaste that has

plenty of _____ and _____ in it.
(plural noun)   (plural noun)

This will help make your teeth _____ and
(color)

_____. When brushing, make sure you use a brush
(adjective)

that has at least _____ bristles. In fact, have two
(two-digit number)

brushes, one for morning and one for night.

Question: How many bristles would that be altogether? _____

Name _____ Date _____

Directions to My House

I'm glad you are able to come over later. We can play

_____ on my new _____.
　　(game)　　　　　　　　　　　　　　(noun)

Here's how to get to my house:

Go _____ miles down
　　　(two-digit number)

_____ Road. Make a
　　(name of person)

right at the _____
　　　　　　　　(adjective)

_____. That's
　　(noun)

_____ Avenue. Go _____
　(name of movie star)　　　　　　　　　(two-digit number)

more miles. Right in front of you will be my _____
　　　　　　　　　　　　　　　　　　　　　　(color)

and _____ house. Watch out for my pet
　　　(color)

_____, _____ !
　　(animal)　　　　　　　(name)

Question: How many miles is it to your house? _____

Name _____ Date _____

My Collection

My great uncle _____ helped me start my
　　　　　　　　　　(name of boy)

_____ collection. I love collecting them
　　(noun)

because they're so _____. My uncle gave me
　　　　　　　　　　(adjective)

_____ to start with. One was very rare. It came
(one-digit number greater than 5)

all the way from _____. I traded that
　　　　　　　　　(place)

one to _____
　　　　(famous person)

for _____
　　(two-digit number)

_____. Then I gave
　　(plural noun)

_____ to my
(one-digit number less than 5)

_____ friend
　　(adjective)

_____.
　(name of person)

Question: How many are left in the collection? _____

Name _____ **Date** _____

Pet Care

_____ make wonderful
(plural noun)

pets. They are _____ and
(adjective)

_____ as well as being easy
(adjective)

to take care of. All you have to do is

change their _____ daily
(plural noun)

and make sure they get plenty of fresh

_____. If they have babies, a typical litter
(plural noun)

will have _____ in it. You might want to give
(two-digit number)

_____ to your best _____. The rest
(one-digit number)   (noun)

you will want to keep.

Question: How many of the pets will you keep? _____

Name _____   Date _____

Crime Report

The wealthy heiress Mrs. Penelope

Fleabiter has reported a serious theft!

As you know, she lives in a

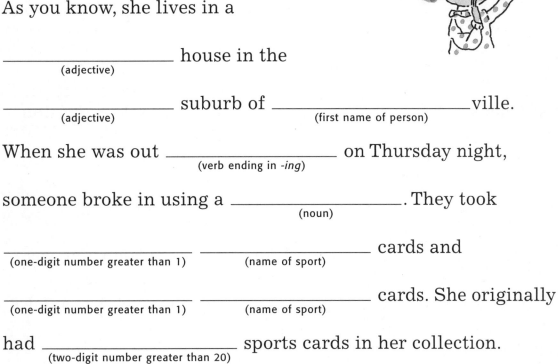

_____ house in the
(adjective)

_____ suburb of _____ville.
(adjective)   (first name of person)

When she was out _____ on Thursday night,
(verb ending in -ing)

someone broke in using a _____. They took
(noun)

_____ _____ cards and
(one-digit number greater than 1)   (name of sport)

_____ _____ cards. She originally
(one-digit number greater than 1)   (name of sport)

had _____ sports cards in her collection.
(two-digit number greater than 20)

Question: How many sports cards does she have left? _____

Name _____ Date _____

Historical Site

You will surely enjoy visiting the historic_____
(first and last name of person)

mansion. It was built in _____out of
(year)

_____ by local _____. One
(plural noun)   (plural noun)

very interesting feature of the house is the windows, because

they were made of _____. This makes the mansion
(plural noun)

look very _____. There were originally
(adjective)

_____ windows on the first floor and
(two-digit number)

_____ on the second floor. When the mansion was
(two-digit number)

renovated, however, _____ windows were covered
(two-digit number less than 20)

over with _____ _____.
(adjective)   (plural noun)

Question: How many windows does the mansion have now? _____

Name _____ Date _____

My Allowance

My dad gives me my allowance every_____
                                                 (day of the week)

at _____, right after he comes home from
         (time)

_____. How much I get depends on what jobs I do.
      (place)

This week I mowed the _____. That was very
                                  (noun)

_____. I get _____ for that. I also
      (adjective)   (money amount less than $5.00)

walked the _____. That's not easy because it
                    (noun)

wouldn't sit still, but I do get _____ for that. That's
                                       (money amount less than $5.00)

all I did, but it was plenty. In fact, Dad was so proud he said I

was _____!
          (adjective)

Question: How much is your allowance this week? _____

Name _____ Date _____

Holiday!

I love it when _____ rolls around in
(name of holiday)

_____. All my relatives including Uncle
(month)

_____, Aunt _____, and even
(name of boy)   (name of girl)

Grandma_____ come over. They always give me
(last name of teacher)

_____ and money! This year my uncle gave me
(plural noun)

_____ _____. My Aunt said, "Don't be
(one-digit number)   (coin, plural)

so _____." She gave me _____
(adjective)   (one-digit number)

_____. My Grandpa gave me _____
(another coin, plural)   (one-digit number)

_____. Then my mom served her famous
(another coin, plural)

_____ cake with lots of _____ on top.
(noun)   (plural noun)

Question: How much money did you get? _____

Name _____   Date _____

Birthday Money

Young _____ just got his birthday money.
(name of boy)

He got _____ _____ dollar bills.
(one-digit even number)   (1, 5, 10, or 20)

He went directly to _____'s
(name of teacher)

Sporting Goods Store. He spent half of

what he had on a new pair of

_____ _____. They
(adjective)   (plural noun)

were _____ and looked really good on his
(color)

_____. He will make good use of them when
(body part)

he plays _____.
(game)

Question: How much birthday money does he have left? _____

Name _____ **Date** _____

Garage Sale

_____ was in the neighborhood and
(name of famous female person)

stopped by my friend _____'s garage sale. She
(name of boy in the class)

had_____ dollars to start with. She bought one of
(two-digit number greater than 30)

his old _____ for _____ dollars. She
(plural noun)   (one-digit number greater than 1)

said she collects them. She also bought two _____.
(plural noun)

She smiled and said they were just

_____. They were
(adjective)

_____ dollars
(one-digit number greater than 1)

each. Then she got into her

_____ and drove
(noun)

off, waving.

Question: **How much did she spend?** _____

Did she get change? _____ **How much?** _____

Name _____   Date _____

My Favorite Restaurant

Yesterday I went to my favorite restaurant,

the _____ _____ .
              (adjective)   (noun)

I ordered my favorite soup, cream of

_____ . It was served just the
       (noun)

way I like it, real _____ and
                           (adjective)

_____ . It cost _____ .
     (adjective)   (price less than $10.00)

I was feeling _____ , so I had roast
                    (adjective)

_____ after that. I think the secret ingredient is
       (noun)

_____ . It was only _____ ! I gave my
    (plural noun)   (price less than $5.00)

favorite waiter, _____ , twenty dollars to pay
                     (name of person)

the bill.

Question: How much change should you get? _____

Name _____ Date _____

History Report

This is a report on King

_____ the First. He
(name of boy in the class)

was King of _____
(place)

from _____ to
(year)

_____. He was very
(later year)

well-respected because of the

way he got rid of _____ so _____.
(plural noun)   (adverb)

When he became king there were _____ in the
(two-digit number)

kingdom. When he retired there were _____ left.
(one-digit number)

That's why people called him _____
(adjective)

and gave him a _____ _____.
(adjective)   (noun)

Question: How many _____ did he get rid of? _____
(same plural noun as above)

Name _____   Date _____

Going Shopping

I love shopping at the mall. When I get

there I always _____ and
        (verb)

_____ first. I eat some
    (verb)

_____, and then I go to my
    (plural noun)

favorite store, _____'s.
            (name of person)

They have the best _____.
                (plural noun)

I love to wear those. They make me look

totally _____. I went there _____
        (adjective)   (one-digit number greater than 1)

times last week and bought _____ of them every
                    (one-digit number greater than 1)

time I went. I am crazy for them, obviously!

Question: How many _____ did you buy? _____
                (plural noun from line 6)

Name _____ Date _____

Secret Agent X

Secret Agent X, also known as _____, is preparing
(name of girl in the class)

for a mission. She went to _____ to see her boss,
(place)

_____, code
(name of teacher in the school)

name: _____
(adjective)

_____. The boss
(name of animal)

said, "You will need to get

_____ suitcases.
(one-digit number greater than 1)

Load up each one with

_____ _____ _____.
(one-digit number greater than 1)　　　　(adjective)　　　　(plural noun)

"Sounds _____. Consider it done," said X.
(adjective)

Question: How many of the _____ does Secret Agent
(same plural noun as above)
X need to get?

Name _____   Date _____

Arms of Steel

So! You want to develop arms of steel.

I, _____, fitness expert, will
    (name of person)

help you. First, you must eat properly.

_____ are good. Have at least
    (plural noun)

_____ every day. Eating them
    (one-digit number)

raw is best. Drink plenty of hot _____, too. You must
                                    (liquid)

also _____. Have good-quality _____
        (verb)   (plural noun)

on your feet for that. Finally, get a large _____.
                                               (noun)

Lift this over your _____ _____ times
                        (body part)   (one-digit number)

every day for a week.

Question: How many times a week should you do your lifts? _____

Name _____   Date _____

The Cousins' Visit

We are going to have a lot of fun this weekend because my

cousins are coming to visit from _____. They
(place)

usually come in their _____-year old car and
(large number)

stay for about _____ days. There are two boys,
(large number)

_____ and _____, and three girls,
(name of boy)   (name of boy)

_____, _____, and _____.
(name of girl)   (name of girl)   (name of girl)

I'm baking my famous _____ _____
(adjective)   (noun)

cookies for them, which I make with fresh _____
(plural noun)

and chocolate-covered _____. I'm making
(plural noun)

_____ of them.
(two-digit number ending in zero)

Question: If you divide the cookies evenly, how many

does each cousin get? _____

Name _____ **Date** _____

Organizing My Room

My mom is making me clean up my room,

just because I left my _____
                          (plural noun)

on the floor and didn't put away my

_____. It's going to take
       (noun)

at least _____
          (number greater than 1)

_____ hours! First, I dusted the
       (adjective)

_____, and then I vacuumed my
       (noun)

_____. Now I have to put away my
       (noun)

_____. I found _____ of them.
       (plural noun)   (two-digit number ending with an even digit)

They've got to be put into two drawers.

Question: How many should you put in each drawer if you

want them to be divided equally? _____

Name _____ Date _____

Candy

My parents are going out tonight to see a new play called

"The _____ _____." I was not happy
    (adjective)   (noun)

that I had to stay home, so I jumped up and down and broke my

_____ in half. My parents gave me a big bag of my
  (noun)

favorite candy, Chewy _____, to calm me down. I
      (plural noun)

have to give half to my babysitter, _____, though.
      (name of teacher)

There are _____ candies in the bag.
  (two-digit even number)

Question: How many pieces of candy will you get? _____

Name _____ **Date** _____

Pizza Dinner

We are having pizza from

_____'s Pizzeria
(name of person)

tonight. I love their pizza. It is so

_____! I like to get it
(adjective)

with _____ and
(plural noun)

_____ on top. I wash
(plural noun)

it down with an extra-large glass of _____.
(liquid)

They cut it into eight slices. I have _____,
(name of teacher)

_____, and _____ coming over to
(name of famous person)   (name of person)

share the pizza with me. We are going to watch a new video, too,

"Revenge of the _____ _____."
(adjective)   (plural noun)

Question: If you divide the pizza evenly, what

fraction of the pizza will you get? _____

Measurement

The fill-in math word problems in this section include math content that supports the math standards for measurement across grades 2–3 (based on the *Principles and Standards for School Mathematics* from the National Council of Teachers of Mathematics) and are organized to accommodate the range of levels you would find in your class. As students complete the blanks in each story, they will build and solve word problems that provide practice in the following areas:

Understand measurable attributes of objects and the units, systems, and processes of measurement and apply appropriate techniques to determine measurements

★ attributes of length, volume, weight, area, and time

★ nonstandard and standard units

★ repetition of a single unit to measure something larger than the unit

★ make comparisons and estimates

★ use formulas to find the area of rectangles

Source: *Principles and Standards for School Mathematics* (National Council of Teachers of Mathematics, 2000); my.nctm.org

Tips for Teaching With This Section

The problems in this section emphasize an understanding of how to combine various standard measurement units such as pints, quarts, inches, ounces, and other common measurements. It's probably not necessary to have measuring tools such as scales and rulers for everyone, but you may want to have one or two appropriate tools to use for demonstrations and to enable students to prove that their answers are correct. It's also helpful when students are working on these problems to supply them with individual measurement reference charts showing names of units of measure, abbreviations, and equivalencies. Or, display a poster containing this information for reference.

Don't forget, time is very much at home in a study of measurement. Help students understand how with time measurements, they can't just add the numbers together and get a sensible answer. For example, if we say John started violin practice at 7:25 on Thursday and practiced for one hour and 45 minutes, to figure out when he finished we can't simply add those numbers, or we would get 8:70! There is no such time. Remind students that with measurements of time, once they have sixty minutes, they need to convert to an hour, very similar to regrouping tens and ones when adding.

Name _____ **Date** _____

Guide to the Famous Tower

When you visit _____ on vacation,
(place)

make sure to bring a _____ because
(noun)

it _____ a lot, and also be sure to
(verb ending in -s)

see the famous tower. When you see the

_____ Tower of _____
(adjective)   (name of person)

you will say, "_____!" The tower is
(exclamation)

_____ inches from the base to the
(two-digit number)

_____. From there to the top it's
(different noun)

_____ feet.
(one-digit number)

Question: How tall is the tower? _____

Name _____ **Date** _____

An Incredible Find!

Well-known archaeologist _____
(first name of boy)

_____ announced an incredible find today. He was
(noun)

exploring the ancient caves of _____. He chipped
(place)

away at a rock wall using his trusty _____ and,
(noun)

underneath some _____, found a _____
(plural noun)   (adjective)

scepter. The scepter is believed to have belonged to Queen

_____. She was famous, of course, for the way she
(first name of girl)

liked to _____ so _____. The handle of
(verb)   (adverb)

the scepter is _____ centimeters long, but it has a
(two-digit number)

sculpture of a _____ _____ on top that
(verb ending in -ing)   (noun)

is another _____ meters long.
(one-digit number)

Question: How long is the scepter all together? _____

Name _____ **Date** _____

The TV Guide

I love to watch TV. My favorite show

is _____ of America. It
$\quad$ (plural noun)

is on channel _____.
$\qquad\qquad$ (two-digit number)

It's so _____. It starts
$\qquad$ (adjective)

at _____ P.M. and lasts _____ minutes.
$\quad$ (time) $\qquad\qquad\qquad$ (two-digit number)

Right after that I watch Wheel of _____. It's a great
$\qquad\qquad\qquad$ (plural noun)

game show. People win _____ prizes like a year's
$\qquad\qquad$ (adjective)

supply of _____ or a trip to _____. The
$\quad$ (plural noun) $\qquad\qquad$ (place)

show is _____ minutes long. When those two are
$\qquad$ (two-digit number)

over, I go right to bed.

Question: What time do you go to bed? _____

Name _____ Date _____

Doing Homework

You know you should always

do your homework so you can be

as _____ as a
     (adjective)

_____ .
    (noun)

_____ is very
 (school subject)

_____ . It should only
   (adjective)

take _____ hours. Do that first. Now, History of
  (one-digit number)

_____ is _____ . It will take
  (plural noun)   (adjective)

_____ hour(s). Finally, you need to read for
 (one-digit number)

_____ minutes in your new assigned book, The
 (two-digit number)

Biography of _____ .
          (first and last name of someone)

Question: How long should your homework take? _____

Name _____   Date _____

What a Chore!

_____!
(exclamation)

_____ had a
(name of boy)

_____ day! He had
(adjective)

major chores to do! First, he had

to _____ his room
(verb)

from _____ to 3 P.M. Then, he had to
(time between noon and 3 P.M.)

_____ the dog from _____ to
(verb)   (time between 3 P.M. and 6 P.M.)

6 P.M. This made him very_____, so he went right to
(adjective)

_____ when he was done.
(place)

Question: How much time did he spend on his chores? _____

Name _____ Date _____

How to Build a

_____ball Court
(adjective)

If you want to build a _____ ball court, here's
(same adjective as in title)

how: First, you need to get a long _____ to measure
(noun)

the rectangular court with. Make sure you have plenty of

_____ because this is _____ work.
(liquid)   (adjective)

Get two of your best _____ to help you, too. The
(plural noun)

length should be _____ feet and the width
(one-digit number greater than 1)

should be _____ feet. You will want to paint an
(one-digit number greater than 1)

out-of-bounds line around the perimeter. Use _____,
(color)

which is the official regulation color.

Question: **What is the perimeter of the court?** _____

Name _____   Date _____

Arts and Crafts

I signed up for the arts and crafts class at _____
                                            (name of famous person)

Elementary School. We are making rugs. I am making mine

out of wool and _____. I have a design of a
                    (plural noun)

_____ _____ sitting on a
        (color)   (noun)

_____ _____ in the middle of my rug.
        (color)   (noun)

My teacher said it looks really _____. She said if I
                                      (adjective)

keep up this kind of work, I'll end up being a _____
                                                    (occupation)

someday. I measured with my _____ and found out
                                   (noun)

my rug was _____ feet long
            (one-digit number greater than 1)

and _____ feet wide.
    (one-digit number greater than 1)

Question: What is the area of your rug? _____

Name _____ Date _____

A Cool Drink

You know how _____ it can
            (adjective)

get in summer. One way to cool off is to mix

up a _____, _____,
         (adjective)   (adjective)

_____ drink! Here's a recipe:
      (adjective)

First get a _____ to mix it in.
                (container)

Use a _____ for stirring. Put in a
            (noun)

_____ of _____ and a
(liquid measurement)   (liquid)

_____ of _____. Mix together, add
(liquid measurement)   (liquid)

_____, and serve.
    (plural noun)

Question: How much does the recipe make? _____

Name _____   Date _____

Bake a Cake

Are you _____? Good! Then you will
          (adjective)

love this cake! When you taste it you will say,

"_____!" In a bowl, put
   (exclamation)

_____   _____
(one-digit number)   (weight measurement)

of _____ and mix
      (plural noun)

in _____
    (one-digit number)

_____ of _____.
(weight measurement)   (plural noun)

This is the batter. _____ the mixture for
                        (verb)

_____ _____. Bake in a
(two-digit number)   (time measurement)

_____ _____ until _____.
   (adjective)   (noun)   (adjective)

Serve on a _____, so it will look nice.
                (noun)

Question: How much batter did you make? _____

Name _____   Date _____

Pirate Gold

A bag of gold was recently found at the

bottom of _____'s Inlet.
                (first name of girl)

It weighed _____
             (one-digit number greater than 1)

pounds. It is suspected that it

originally belonged to a pirate

named Peg-_____ _____. He was
              (body part)   (first name of boy)

known for always _____ his beard before he sailed
                   (verb ending in -ing)

his _____, and for his parrot, _____.
        (noun)   (name)

The diver who found the gold, Mr. _____
                                    (first name of boy)

_____, will get to keep _____ ounces.
     (noun)   (one-digit number greater than 1)

The rest will go to the Museum of Ancient _____.
                                             (plural noun)

Question: How much gold will the museum get? _____

Geometry

The fill-in math word problems in this section include math content that supports the math standards for geometry across grades 2–3 (based on the *Principles and Standards for School Mathematics* from the National Council of Teachers of Mathematics) and are organized to accommodate the range of levels you would find in your class. As students complete the blanks in each story, they will build and solve word problems that provide practice in the following areas:

Analyze characteristics and properties of two- and three-dimensional geometric shapes and develop mathematical arguments about geometric relationships
- ★ two- and three-dimensional shapes
- ★ subdividing, combining, and transforming shapes
- ★ congruence and similarity
- ★ geometric properties and relationships

Apply transformations and use symmetry to analyze mathematical situations
- ★ recognize and apply slides, flips, and turns
- ★ symmetry

Use visualization, spatial reasoning, and geometric modeling to solve problems
- ★ create mental images of geometric shapes
- ★ recognize and represent shapes from different perspectives

Source: *Principles and Standards for School Mathematics* (National Council of Teachers of Mathematics, 2000); my.nctm.org

Tips for Teaching With This Section

As students work to solve the problems in this section, consider the following strategies:

- ★ Students will benefit from having reference charts available, either personal sheets or large charts containing shape names and information (including diagrams).

- ★ Make students aware that people who work with geometric ideas, such as architects and designers (as well as mathematicians), are always writing and drawing as they solve problems. Encourage students to recognize that trying to solve a problem in their head can lead them to lose track of some of the requirements or data. Drawing a picture and recording information are always a good idea. (For more problem-solving strategies, see pages 7–8.)

- ★ Use of manipulatives, such as pattern blocks and attribute blocks, is also helpful for students who have difficulty visualizing combinations of shapes that might be required to solve some of these problems. Another useful manipulative both in measurement (with perimeter and area) and working on geometric-based problems is a geoboard and rubber bands. Students can follow the problem and create the shapes as they process the facts in each problem.

Name _____ Date _____

The Garden

If you are planning a garden, here is

some _____ advice.
　　　　　(adjective)

Make sure you have plenty of

_____. Spread them
　　(plural noun)

_____ over the ground.
　　(adverb)

Put a high fence around all

_____ sides of the garden. This is to keep
(one-digit even number greater than 2)

out the _____ _____. You know they
　　　　　(adjective)　　　　　　　　(plural noun)

like to _____ the _____.
　　　　　(verb)　　　　　　　(plural noun)

Question: What shape is your garden? _____

Name _____   Date _____

Hat Shopping

I need a new hat because I am going to my uncle

_____'s wedding. We were surprised he is getting
(name of boy)

married because he is _____ years old. The wedding
(number)

is in _____. It will be a very _____
(place)   (adjective)

wedding because my cousin is a famous _____. The
(occupation)

hat has to match my _____. I think
(noun)

_____ and _____ would look good.
(color)   (color)

The shape of the hat should have _____
(number greater than 2 but less than 7)

sides. People will see it and say, "Oh _____, that hat
(exclamation)

is looking _____!"
(adjective)

Question: What shape will your hat be? _____

Name _____ Date _____

The Sculpture

Famous sculptor _____
(name of girl in the class)

is starting a new _____
(adjective)

masterpiece. Her last sculpture was

made of _____ and
(plural noun)

_____. The critics said it
(plural noun)

was _____. This time she
(adjective)

is going to use geometric shapes. She has _____
(one-digit number greater than 1)

_____ and _____
(geometric shape, plural)   (one-digit number greater than 1)

_____. On top she will put a _____.
(geometric shape, plural)   (geometric shape)

Question: What will her new sculpture look like? Draw it.

Name _____   Date _____

Chef Bob's Creation

Chef Bob is hard at work at his new

restaurant, the _____
                        (adjective)

_____. His new dessert
      (noun)

makes people _____ with
                    (verb)

delight. The bottom is shaped like a

_____ and is made of
   (geometric shape)

_____. It is covered with
   (plural noun)

_____. It has _____
   (plural noun)   (one-digit number greater than 1)

_____ shaped like _____ on top. One
   (plural noun)   (geometric shape, plural)

taste and you will say, "This is like eating _____."
                                                      (plural noun)

Question: What does Chef Bob's new dessert look like? Draw it.

Name _____ Date _____

The New Playground

Our town finally built a new playground. It is

mostly made of _____ and
       (plural noun)

_____. Of course there
  (plural noun)

are _____ to slide
     (plural noun)

down and _____ to
          (plural noun)

climb. It's always _____ to _____ on
                    (adjective)   (verb)

those. In the center there's a _____. It has a picture
                               (noun)

of the mayor painted on it. His eyes are _____ and
                                         (geometric shape, plural)

his nose is a _____. His head is actually shaped like
              (geometric shape)

a _____!
  (geometric shape)

Question: What does the mayor look like? Draw his portrait, and then draw a line of symmetry through it.

Patterns and Algebra

The fill-in math word problems in this section include math content that supports the math standards for algebra across grades 2–3 (based on the *Principles and Standards for School Mathematics* from the National Council of Teachers of Mathematics) and are organized to accommodate the range of levels you would find in your class. As students complete the blanks in each story, they will build and solve word problems that provide practice in the following areas:

Understand patterns, relations, and functions
★ sort, classify, and order objects by size, number, and other properties
★ recognize, describe, extend, and make generalizations about patterns
★ use words, tables, and graphs to represent and analyze patterns

Represent and analyze mathematical situations and structures using algebraic symbols
★ principles and properties of operations (such as commutativity)
★ invented and conventional symbolic notations
★ properties of commutativity, associativity, and distributivity
★ missing variables
★ express mathematical relationships using equations

Use mathematical models to represent and understand quantitative relationships
★ use objects, pictures, and symbols to model situations involving addition and subtraction of whole numbers
★ model problems with objects; use graphs, tables, and equations to draw conclusions

Source: *Principles and Standards for School Mathematics* (National Council of Teachers of Mathematics, 2000); my.nctm.org

Tips for Teaching With This Section

Finding patterns help us make predictions about what comes next. Patterns and Algebra is another area of mathematics in which taking information from a problem and writing it down in the form of a list or table is extremely helpful. Share the following strategies with students as they work with the problems in this section:

★ Potentially confusing patterns can be made easier when the numbers are taken out of the word context and arranged in a logical way. Encourage students to arrange numbers in organized rows, columns, or streams that are near each other so that relationships between the numbers can be easily detected. For example, if we are looking for a pattern of raisins being eaten by children, we could organize the data like this:

1 child	10 raisins
2 children	20 raisins
3 children	30 raisins

If someone asked how many raisins nine children would eat, we could answer 90 by extending the relationship between the number of children and the number of raisins eaten-in this case, the number of children multiplied by 10 or, using algebra, $n \times 10 =$ raisins eaten. This is a growing pattern, where the numbers increase.

★ Students may also encounter repeating patterns, where the elements of the pattern don't grow but simply repeat, as with the mail carrier who wears blue socks on odd days and red socks on even days, and we want to know what color socks he will be wearing on Thursday if Monday is July 10. (answer = blue, because Thursday would be July 13, which is an odd numbered day)

Name _____ Date _____

Message From the Cave

_____ scientists from the University of
(adjective)

_____ have recently discovered a cave filled with
(place)

ancient _____. Not only that, there were drawings
(plural noun)

on the cave walls, too. Everything was in a straight line. First,

there were three _____, followed by two
(plural noun)

_____, a _____, and
(plural noun)   (noun)

_____ _____. Then the whole thing
(one-digit number greater than 1)   (plural noun)

repeated.

Question: What is the pattern on the cave wall? Draw it.

Name _____   **Date** _____

Aliens Speak!

I was reading my favorite newspaper,

the National _____ yesterday.
                    (noun)

The headline said that a man received

messages from aliens from the planet

_____. The message said that the aliens are coming
    (first name of person)

to Earth because they need more _____ to survive.
                                        (plural noun)

Without them, they cannot _____. They would have
                                    (verb)

to _____ _____ instead. Their message
        (verb)   (plural noun)

was a number pattern. It said: _____,
                                    (odd number less than 3)

_____, _____,
(even number less than 3)   (number of triangle sides)

_____.
(even number greater than 2 but less than 5)

Question: What would be a good clue for the next number in the

pattern? _____

_____

_____

Name _____   **Date** _____

Big Winner

_____ is a big winner!
(name of girl)

Some people say she looks a lot like

_____ and is as smart as
(name of female celebrity)

_____. She was on that
(name of teacher)

famous game show, Who Wants to Be a

_____? She won one dollar
(noun)

in the first round. She won

_____ dollars in the third round. Her total winnings
(two-digit number)

were _____ after three _____ rounds.
(three-digit number)   (adjective)

Question: How much money did she win in round two? _____

Name _____   Date _____

The Big Sale

_____'s Super
(name of person)

Saver Store is having its

annual _____
(animal)

Day sale! I really want to buy

a new _____.
(noun)

My old one is too small for me.

I want to get a _____ one with _____
(color)   (color)

trim this time. I've saved _____ dollar(s), but it
(one-digit number less than 5)

costs _____ dollars.
(number greater than 6 but less than 20)

Question: How much more money do you need? _____

Name _____ Date _____

The Scientific Lecture

Dr. _____
(first name of girl)

_____ was giving a
(noun)

lecture at _____
(noun)

College. She was very happy to be

asked to speak at such a _____ place. Her topic was
(adjective)

Measuring the Speed of _____. "First," she said, "you
(plural noun)

must measure it with a(n) _____ _____."
(adjective)   (noun)

She demonstrated for the students. She found that it was

_____ inches long. "I now know that the
(even number greater than 8 but less than 12)

maximum speed would be 100 mph. I simply multiplied the

length by the speed factor X.

Question: What is X? _____

Data Analysis and Probability

The fill-in math word problems in this section include math content that supports the math standards for data analysis and probability across grades 2–3 (based on the *Principles and Standards for School Mathematics* from the National Council of Teachers of Mathematics) and are organized to accommodate the range of levels you would find in your class. As students complete the blanks in each story, they will build and solve word problems that provide practice in the following areas:

Select and use appropriate statistical methods to analyze data

★ describe the data; determine what the data show

★ compare related data sets (including how the data are distributed)

Develop and evaluate inferences and predictions that are based on data; understand and apply basic concepts of probability

★ discuss events as likely or unlikely

★ propose and justify conclusions and predictions based on data

★ predict the probability of outcomes

Source: *Principles and Standards for School Mathematics* (National Council of Teachers of Mathematics, 2000); my.nctm.org

Tips for Teaching With This Section

Remind students to consider the following strategies when working on problems with data:

★ Make a list or table to organize information or data from the word problem. (For more problem-solving strategies, see pages 7–8.) This makes it easier to compare, arrange, and think about the facts.

★ Labeling data with units or word labels also helps keep things organized and the numbers meaningful. If the problem talks about cats and dogs, encourage students to label the numbers that appear as either being cats or dogs. When students write "naked numbers" on a page, they sometimes forget what those numbers stand for.

★ Think about how you can use numbers such as fractions to represent probabilities. For example, if there are four red marbles in a bag and one blue one, the chance of getting a blue marble can be described as being 1/5 or one out of five. Once again, labeling helps maintain meaning in these problems.

Name _____   Date _____

Soccer Stars

Soccer has become a very

_____ game with many
(adjective)

_____ because it is
(plural noun)

_____ , _____ ,
(adjective)   (adjective)

and _____ . Recently, a
(adjective)

three-day goal-scoring competition was

held in _____ .
(name of country)

_____ scored two goals each day of the competition.
(name of movie star)

_____ scored one goal the first day, two the second,
(name of singer)

and three on the third.

Question: Of these two players, who scored more goals? _____

Name _____   Date _____

The Contest

_____ and
(name of boy in the class)

_____ are going to
(name of famous female)

have a contest. Whoever can eat the

most _____ in two
(plural noun)

days is the winner. You know

how _____ they are
(adjective)

(especially when covered with _____)! Our male
(plural noun)

contestant ate _____ the first day and
(one-digit number greater than 1)

_____ the second day. Our female contestant ate
(one-digit number)

_____ more than he did on the first day, but one less
(one-digit number)

than he did on the second day.

Question: Who won the contest? _____

Name _____   Date _____

Baseball Hero

Baseball's leading hitter, _____, has had another
                            (name of girl)

_____ season. Of course she uses a bat made of
   (adjective)

specially seasoned _____, so that helps. In May she
                         (noun)

got _____ hits. In June she got _____.
    (one-digit number)   (one-digit number)

July was the same as June, and then in August she felt really

_____ and got _____ hits. She says she
   (adjective)   (one-digit number)

gets her _____ hitting power from eating plenty of
        (adjective)

_____ and drinking lots of _____.
   (plural noun)   (liquid)

Question: How many hits did she average per month? _____

Name _____ Date _____

The Probability _____
(container)

I hope you are feeling very _____, because now it's
(adjective)

time for the very _____ Probability _____.
(adjective)   (same container as above)

Inside we will place _____ _____
(one-digit number greater than 1)   (adjective)

_____. We will also place _____
(plural noun)   (one-digit number greater than 1)

_____ _____. Now you get to close
(adjective)   (plural noun)

your eyes, reach in, and pick one out.

Question: What is the probability of picking

one of the first group of items? _____

Name _____   Date _____

County Fair

Princess _____ went
        (first name of girl in the class)

to the _____
        (first name of someone in the class)

County Fair. There were rides like the

Tilt-a- _____ and games
            (noun)

like Toss a _____. The
                (noun)

princess decided to play a new game

called _____'s Lucky Pick.
        (first name of boy in the class)

In this game the dealer lays out _____ cards
                                  (one-digit number greater than 3)

facedown. One is a _____, two are
                        (noun)

_____, and the rest are aces.
    (plural noun)

Question: What are the princess's chances of picking an ace? _____